TO TASTE THE WATER

FIRST SERIES: POETRY

For Barbara —
New friend on this strange and beautiful journey ~

To Taste the Water

Yours,

Poems by
Norman Minnick

MID-LIST PRESS
Minneapolis

October, Earlham
2010

Copyright © 2000, 2001, 2002, 2003, 2005, 2006, and 2007 by Norman Minnick.
All rights reserved.
Published by Mid-List Press 4324 12th Avenue South
Minneapolis, Minnesota 55407-3218.
Visit our website at www.midlist.org.

Mid-List Press publishes books of high literary merit and fresh artistic vision by new and emerging writers and by writers ignored, marginalized, or excluded from publication by commercial and mainstream publishers. Mid-List seeks to increase access to publication for new writers, to nurture the growth of emerging writers, and, generally, to increase the diversity of books, authors, and readers. Mid-List Press is a tax-exempt, 501(c)(3), not-for-profit literary organization.

Library of Congress Cataloging-in-Publication Data
Minnick, Norman, 1970–
 To taste the water : poems / by Norman Minnick.
  p. cm.
 "First series—poetry."
 ISBN 978-0-922811-74-8 (trade pbk. : alk. paper)
 I. Title.
PS3613.I65T6 2007
811'.6—dc22

2007019909

Manufactured in the United States
First printing: August 2007
Cover photo: *Maple at Pike Island* by Mark Kawell. Copyright © 2007 Mark Kawell.
Text and cover design: Lane Stiles

for LeAnn, Miranda and Dustin

CONTENTS

Stacking Dishes in the Early Morning   3
Her Inheritance   4
The Silence between Notes (1)   5
The Blind   7
Her Image   8
Pissarro's *The House of the Deaf Woman and the Belfry at Eragny*   9
Stranded   10
While You Work   11
Ingres's Valpinçon Bather   12
Things That Fly   13
The Gift   16
Migration   17
The Current   18
Our Guide   19
Chinese Art   20
Poem between Basho and Levertov   22
Hands   23
Waiting Room   24
How Poetry Comes to Me   25
Matters of Speaking   26
Unfathomable Depth   28
Falling Asleep   29
Three Small Poems about My Father   30
Reading *Little Red–Cap* to My Daughter   31
Forever Becoming   32
The Silence between Notes (2)   33
Annuals   35
Another Peace Rally   36
Bainbridge, Indiana   37
Pay Attention   38

Walking Along the Edge of the Woods at Dusk My Daughter
Asks about God Again   39
Blue, Green, a Hint of Yellow   40
The Sandpiper   41
A Man Drives Many Miles   42
The Busy Street   43
Scene   44
Initiation   45
It Wasn't Until I Reached the Age My Father Was When He
Took Me to See the Ocean That I Realized It Had Been His
First Time Too   46
The Great Wind   47

Acknowledgments   49

*Water, by what hidden channel have you come
welling up with a new life
I had not tasted before?*

—Antonio Machado

STACKING DISHES IN THE EARLY MORNING

This is how
    the earth did it,

I imagine,
    slowly,

with as much care,
    over a billion years,

carefully placing
    layer upon layer

so not to disturb
    the entire stack;

so not to disturb
    the woman rising softly

from the warm layers
    of another room.

HER INHERITANCE

    Give a child
paper and crayons
and she will
recreate the world.
            Do you know why
she comes into your room at night
complaining she is thirsty?
Why she can't sleep?
She has tried to write her name, to draw
an ocean, but keeps encountering
the edge of the page.
          Tell her the sky
is meant for her.
           Tell her the clouds
are to drink from.
           Tell her the story
of a husband and wife
who sailed beyond the horizon
only to find another horizon, and beyond that . . .
           Let her hear the waves
lapping at the side of the boat.
          Let her feel the rocking motion.
          Let her know
that steadiness is essential
as Hölderlin says, that we need
to learn to live swaying
as in a rocking boat
on the sea.

THE SILENCE BETWEEN NOTES (1)

The first flakes of snow float
all afternoon.

By morning
the road home
will have disappeared.

∾

In Beethoven's "Hammerklavier"
a third hand appears.

The composer sits alone
in the wide expanse between hands,

reaches out and touches
the foot of God.

∾

Live like the vine that
climbs the tree without
touching the tree.

∾

All night rain.
Daffodils grow tall
as children.

∾

An echo
has no choice in the matter.

∽

When coyote comes toward you
confuse him by sniffing his ass.

∽

Water once flowed
where stones gather.

∽

Poetry, if good, should make you forget
the music in your head.

∽

When I sit down to Beethoven
my fingers tremble before
touching the keys.

THE BLIND

If you dedicated your life to a forest,
no one would blame you.

And it wouldn't be your fault
if you became lost.

It would be admirable to enter that forest,

but there are folds of darkness that
only the blind man accepts.

It would be okay to take him as your guide.

Be ready!
On the other side is a view like no other.

The blind man will ask you to describe it.

HER IMAGE

    My daughter,
    captivated
    by her inverse image
    in the curve of a spoon,
    turns it over and back
    and over again,
    and back again,
    her image
    upside down,
    right side up,
    faster, as if she might
    trick the spoon.

    Eat, I tell her.

PISSARRO'S *THE HOUSE OF THE DEAF WOMAN AND THE BELFRY AT ERAGNY*

What he really wants to paint
is behind him,

but the solitary sound of a bell
at the wrong hour turns him
toward the belfry.

It is a song he can no longer
avoid. But it isn't only
the mournful song of a bell
that calls to him,

it is the cloud's lament, the ripe
agony of trees, grass,
all living things.

He knows nature is so mysterious
he cannot embrace it.

Nothing is immobile.
Nothing is without sound.

He knows that a canvas that does not shimmer
will not stir even one fiber
of his soul.

Only Pissarro paints a music
so mournful, so beautiful
it can make a deaf woman
fall to her knees.

STRANDED

Are we here
to give the sea
the assurance it needs
to reflect
the sheer austerity of the sky?

Is the sea here
to remind us
how small we really are,

torn between mysteries
beyond the horizon
and the abundance
of the land?

The waves
call us to a greater depth.

A sound
from among trees
calls us to reason
with the wind.

Give us a few planks of wood,
a strong thread
and a powerful storm.

We have never been
stranded before.

WHILE YOU WORK

    While you sit at your desk
water striders dance upon the surface of a pond,
high, thin clouds stretch across the sky,
and acres of tall grass, reticent after a long dry summer,
practice nothing but grace.

INGRES'S VALPINÇON BATHER

I have seen her many times,
her back turned, with something in her arms
she doesn't want me to see.

Is it a bowl of water? A guitar?
    If I could guess the right thing
she would show her face.
Ingres would be delighted to know
that he perfected the art of light and shade.

And I, brushing her sloping shoulder
ever so lightly, would slip past her
into the dark recess of the room,
beyond the pouring water.

In another dream
she dries herself in the moonlight.

THINGS THAT FLY

I

The loon laughing at the night
has a much darker calling.

The whippoorwill takes all she is given
and turns it into a simple melody.

The waxwing, drunk on the luscious juice of overripe juniper berries,
cannot lift its body off the ground.

The American bittern—the poor American bittern—stands petrified,
her bill pointed straight to the sky to prove that
she is protected by a higher power.

These are songs of things that fly—
living things with little attachment
to the earth,

giving themselves
to the wind,

reinventing flight
each time they take to the air.

2

I woke one morning to a lawn full of egrets
and could not make sense of that scene,

so I became one of them. How glorious it felt to be
on the outside looking in.

It was December. Boca Raton. Warm sun.
I could smell the sea.

I thought of those I left behind in the cold and snow.
Thoughts such as these make one human again.

3

I wanted to find a poem in what's hidden.

Outside my window
a nest of robins
mouths open
heads thrust to the sky.

Their mother arrived
placed something still alive
at the backs of their throats.

That night
drifting in and out of delicious sleep
the poem I could not write came to life
at the back of my throat
and by dawn had learned to fly.

THE GIFT

for Sara Sant'Ambrogio

The cellist,
Beethoven still in her hands,
touches my daughter's hands
and tells her how perfect they are
for an aspiring cellist.

My daughter smiles,
blushes a little. She has no idea
what she now holds.

MIGRATION

    The sun has nothing left to say.
    The grass breathes a slow sigh of relief.
    All day I have been raking leaves.
    Now, as evening approaches, my attention
    is called to the sky. Geese
    call to one another across their perfect form.
    The last one turns its head and looks at me. It wonders
    how I live my life and neither lead nor follow.

THE CURRENT

> *for Stanley Kunitz on his 100th birthday*

At first I thought to pick up the phone
and call you. But you don't know me.
So I took your book,
snuck out of the office, and sat on the grass
in the shadow of a white ash
beside this derelict canal.

Built in the 1830s
it was supposed to connect
the Wabash Canal with the Erie Canal.
Then the railroads came.

After reading aloud
a few of my favorite poems,
I looked into the water.

A bluegill swam against the current, turned
perpendicular to the shore
and allowed the current
to push it back to where it began.

It did this over and over again.

It must have been at play.
What else could it do?

OUR GUIDE

Our canoe glides easily
through the water.

This river is slow.
It keeps us going.

A great blue heron
flops lazily down the river,
its feet at times touching the surface,
settles for a moment on a low branch
and waits for us.

CHINESE ART

A sparrow hangs
upside down from a limb,
beak open,
calling from below
for change.

꩜

Wang Xia loved to drink.
He dipped his long hair
into black ink and
flung it on the silk
kicking and shouting,
laughing and singing.

When sober
he made from the disorder
mountains, streams, rocks,
gullies, clouds,
rain.

꩜

Three children play
under Ming dynasty trees
in the underglaze
of a lotus-shaped jar
containing everything
and nothing.

꩜

Two crows
perch on the same
thin branch, in the same
empty world.
One is looking away,
laughing.

A single branch cannot
handle the weight
of two crows laughing.

POEM BETWEEN BASHO AND LEVERTOV

"Don't follow in the footsteps of the old poets,
seek what they sought."
   —Matsuo Basho

She wants me to cut
straight through the middle of the apple
so she can see the star at its core.

"This is the year the old ones,
the old great ones
leave us alone on the road . . ."
   —Denise Levertov

HANDS

I have stood close to death
and still don't know what to do with my hands
at a crowded funeral.

They give comfort
to the darkness inside pockets

but swim frantically
when someone places their hand on my shoulder
and turns me toward the door.

As the coffin is closed
a voice in cold air says
it is time to go.

WAITING ROOM

All around me people are dying.
An old tune set to Muzak
becomes the soundtrack
to our despair. Beside me,
an old woman,
her right hand spread
long and narrow on her husband's knee
like a speckled trout thrown from the river,
her left clutching a tissue in her lap.
She says to her husband, *I'll tell you
when to worry.* This comforts me
as I search for a better life
in a well-traveled magazine
trying not to look up,
trying not to touch
its wrinkled pages.

HOW POETRY COMES TO ME

(after Snyder)

Seek not, a voice says.

I open my eyes to total darkness
and for a moment forget where I am.

When the lamp is not there,
a tremor runs the length of my body.

Outside my tent
something moves, and I can't remember
whether to play dead
or make myself appear
as large as possible.

MATTERS OF SPEAKING

    1

It matters what you say.
It matters which way the animal retreats.
It matters what you don't say.

    2

Sometimes when I open my mouth
out comes a fist.

    3

I wish I could speak
in parables,

but more often
I am like a sprinkler in the rain,

so much
already being said
that the earth becomes saturated

and can no longer accept
what I say.

4

The embers sing.
We stand unmoving,
cheeks and eyes burning.

5

Two sides to everything.

Then there is a smoldering fire, silent dawn, mound of ashes.

6

It matters if you sing.
It matters if you do not sing.
It matters if you listen or do not listen.

7

It matters if you follow the animal.

UNFATHOMABLE DEPTH

Walking along the shore at night
I came upon a turtle brooding in the sand.

The waves came in slowly. The moon bright.
We were alone

so I sat next to her
and told her about my life. I felt warm.
I said:

Some people,
no matter what you give them
still want the moon . . .

How patient she was sitting beside me in the sand
while I recited great poems by the sea!

And when I saw the moon I fell silent,
then stood and followed it into the sea
deeper than I had ever been.

FALLING ASLEEP

The eyes know.
The heartbeat
slows. Thoughts blur
and limbs become
useless.

A beautiful stranger
crosses the dance floor
mysterious and graceful,
takes me by the arm
and whispers, *Don't worry,
I'll lead.*

THREE SMALL POEMS ABOUT MY FATHER

1

My father says he'll know
in which direction we are traveling
when he finds the moss on a tree.
*Which side does the moss grow on? I ask.
The north, he replies.*
And we drive. The road winding.

2

We come to a fork in the road.
I begin to quote Frost
but he quotes Yogi Berra first:
*When you come to a fork in the road . . .
take it.* The rest of the way we talk
baseball.

3

The twigs are too damp to burn,
the fire hesitant. My father
breathes on it. The flames,
as if startled, jump
into the air. *All it needs
is a little help,* he says.
And we stand side by side
breathing into the fire.
Our shadows stretch for miles
into the indelible night.

READING *LITTLE RED–CAP* TO MY DAUGHTER

The wolf swallows his victims
whole, too greedy, too gluttonous
to bother chewing. Then
full and fat he sleeps.
She smiles. Scissors are used
to cut him open.
Oh, she says.
Those who were eaten are reborn
and can breathe on their own.
They are replaced
by stones
and the wolf is sewn back up.
She looks a little pale.
The wolf becomes
thirsty, drags himself
to the well.
She sees where *this* is going.

FOREVER BECOMING

A man is dying of thirst.

He tastes water on the air and he believes
that just over the ridge a shimmering body of water waits
for him.

In time
he finds himself
face to face
with the most magnificent creature he has ever seen.

He dips his hands into the cold water and drinks
while deep within him another thirst is growing—
a darker thirst.

A man is dying of thirst for himself.
His body is swollen with darkness.

This man who has fallen in love with himself drinks
and drinks again
filling himself
with himself
quenching an
undying thirst, a thirst
he never had for the world.

THE SILENCE BETWEEN NOTES (2)

We walk through the orchard
discussing Nietzsche . . .

apples that have fallen on the ground are being eaten
from the inside out.

↜

I know the sound of stone hitting water.
How can I accept this sinking feeling?

↜

Remember, Hades abducted Persephone
in broad daylight.

↜

If need is music
and desire the silence between notes,
what are we listening to?

↜

Don't tell me your troubles.
I've seen fish in the deepest caves
who have no use for eyes.

↜

When coyote comes toward you
you better have something in your hand.

∽

William Stafford says:
"Your job is to find what the world is trying to be."

∽

When will we be setting places at the table
for our weaknesses?

∽

We took our oars
walked back toward the sea
and set off.

In order to return we will
have to settle
the differences between us.

ANNUALS

The petunias you planted last year
weren't supposed to bloom again.

Across the street
a woman waves excitedly
from inside her house.
I wave back. She is cleaning her windows
and doesn't see me.

Suddenly I am inside the house I grew up in,
sitting cross-legged on the bare floor of the living room
looking at dust and crumbs
that have gathered between boards.

It is dusk. Those flowers
are more brilliant now than before.

All day they tried to hold
our attention. All day they stood together
against the wind.

ANOTHER PEACE RALLY

A twice-
wounded Vietnam
veteran leads us
in a chant that goes,
One, two, three, four . . .
and, as if it couldn't
get worse, *We don't want
your stinkin' war!*
When the cage is opened,
twenty-four doves flap upward
into the cool air.
Can those who support our failing
not see how those birds
give themselves to the wind?
Can they not see our children
who can't keep their eyes off those birds
as behind tall buildings
they circle and disappear?

BAINBRIDGE, INDIANA

Sitting at the corner of Cherry and Main
in Bainbridge, Indiana, I hear the hum
of an ice machine beside the BP.

A hawk soars overhead, its right wing
missing a few feathers.

Someone has shot five holes in the stop sign,
missing all four letters.

A small, white house sits comfortably
on its half acre, the windows open.
A curtain billows out from one.

There's no sound but the ice machine
and a few birds somewhere high in a tree.

PAY ATTENTION

All my life I have been told
to pay attention, stop daydreaming,
pay attention, keep up, pay
attention, get to work. So much emphasis
on the word *pay*, now I am broke, my mind crowded
and noisy. Guests that were not invited
will not leave. I am interested in this word
attention.

I step outside for fresh air.
Moon and owl compete
for the highest branch of a sugar maple.

WALKING ALONG THE EDGE OF THE WOODS AT DUSK MY DAUGHTER ASKS ABOUT GOD AGAIN

God is in everything, I tell her,
hoping the mystery and matter-of-factness
will give her something to think about.
Everything? Everything.
The clouds? The grass?
What about the dirt?
What about me? What about
you? And before I can answer
a great horned owl,
almost as tall as my daughter,
looks at us.
It extends its massive wings
and with one downward thrust
lifts its body
and disappears, leaving
a small lump of fur and broken bones
in the dark grass.

BLUE, GREEN, A HINT OF YELLOW

Fog fills the narrow spaces
between houses.

A black Lab leaps about
snapping at the moist, delicious air.

I close the notebook on its empty pages
and walk without destination

into the thickness hoping something
speaks to me.

The cold white disk of the sun perhaps,
or the stones that own this low wall.

A crow drops and floats beside me,
turns and perches on the frozen earth,

and I see that, even in this pale light, the crow
is not entirely black.

THE SANDPIPER

        The sandpiper
        is always
on the move.
It's odd.
When the tide
        brings the food in
        it's funny how
the sandpiper
works so hard
        for so little.
        The sandpiper
        doesn't complain
of back pain
or muscle cramps,
doesn't have
        a lawyer.
        What the sandpiper knows
        that we don't know
        is how
not to get wet.

A MAN DRIVES MANY MILES

    A man drives many miles before he stops,
    gets out, and runs down the road
    until his car is no longer in sight.

    He is stopped by something invisible,
    a scent perhaps, which reminds him
    of the small town of his youth,
    or something he wanted to say years ago.

    The familiar freshness of morning
    turns the man in the direction from which he came.

        Suppose he left the door ajar,
        would the warmth of his earlier presence remain?

    If he ran back toward the car
    past trees full of laughter,
    he would remember days he wanted to forget.

    If he ran forward,
    he would fall in love with a woman
    who would caress his broken jaw,

    and he would come to hate the fist
    balled up in his throat.

THE BUSY STREET

Who is he walking alone
who claims to mind his own business
as the wind sweeps him along into another body—

an uncomfortable body with cold feet
and hands too dirty to shield his eyes
from flying debris?

Is he the boy who wanders off in class
and sits down to share his lunch with the pigeons?

Is he the nervous boy who loosens his tie to stand off-key
in the strange arena below Emily Dickinson's
        window?

Or is he the young man ready to step into the street
of rushing traffic, calling to a woman

who disappears behind a bus, moving?

SCENE

    Sun sets behind mountain.
    I want to describe it to you.
    But your face when I say nothing!
    The mountain inside the mountain!

INITIATION

A fisherman plods through deep sand
to catch his pole as it curls to the sea.

A crowd has gathered on the shore. A giant fish
leaps into the air. The man fights hard. His hands are slipping.

The fish leaps again and again, sunlight glinting
off its silver body. The man is on his knees, his face is red.

He holds his breath and pulls the fish in
wrestling it to the shore.

The crowd turns and goes home, all save

a small child who has just discovered
the full capacity of his lungs.

IT WASN'T UNTIL I REACHED THE AGE MY FATHER WAS WHEN HE TOOK ME TO SEE THE OCEAN THAT I REALIZED IT HAD BEEN HIS FIRST TIME TOO

He was too captivated
by the wide
blue mouth that welcomed him home
to mind my short legs
that could barely keep up.

We ran fully clothed
into the sea.
It will be our ritual!
he said, and together
we drank.

Astonished
by its offensive bite
I looked up and witnessed
my father
interrogating the waves.

Back on shore
I saw myself rocking
in my mother's arms
like a skiff full
of emigrants
and secrets.

THE GREAT WIND

> *How clean, how beautiful the great wind was.*
> —Robert Francis

A great wind came and claimed everything.

I have stood in this doorway for years
looking upon its wake—amazed by what it took:

the car, the mailbox, the dog on his chain;
it came and took everything—

the neighbor, the neighbor's dog and the neighbor's tree,
the tree by my window and the owl who watched me howl in my sleep,

and all the birds in all the trees along the street. It took everything—
the road and the grass and the water from the spring,

the highway and the church and even the YMCA.

It was angry and came without warning—
took the seasons, the war, yesterday and tomorrow.

It came swiftly and took the clouds and the graves,
heaven and hell.

And sadness! It even took sadness!

But there was one thing left, clinging to the frame of the door,
having nearly gone unnoticed:

a wet leaf like the small hand of a child.

ACKNOWLEDGMENTS

Grateful acknowledgment is made to the editors of the following print and online publications in which these poems previously appeared: *Blue Mesa Review*, "Hunger"; *Can We Have Our Ball Back*, "Hands"; *The Caribbean Writer*, "It Wasn't Until I Reached the Age My Father Was When He Took Me to See the Ocean That I Realized It Had Been His First Time Too"; *Chelsea*, "Forever Becoming," "Pissarro's *The House of the Deaf Woman and the Belfry at Eragny*," "The Silence between Notes," "Things That Fly"; *The Christian Science Monitor*, "Three Small Poems about My Father"; *Diner*, "Stacking Dishes in the Early Morning"; *Ekphrasis*, "Ingres's Valpinçon Bather"; *Exquisite Corpse*, "The Sandpiper"; *The Grove Review*, "Matters of Speaking"; *Heliotrope*, "Initiation," "Blue, Green, a Hint of Yellow"; *Maize*, "The Blind," "Hands," "Stranded"; *Mangrove*, "The Great Wind"; *Notre Dame Review*, "The Busy Street"; *Open 24 Hours*, "Forever Becoming," "Her Inheritance"; *Poetry Bay*, "A Man Drives Many Miles"; *Poiesis*, "Her Inheritance"; *The Seattle Review*, "Unfathomable Depth"; *Spillway*, "How Poetry Comes to Me"; and *The Texas Observer*, "The Sandpiper."

"Pissarro's *The House of the Deaf Woman and the Belfry at Eragny*" won the Poetry in the Gallery competition sponsored by the Indianapolis Museum of Art in 2003. "Migration" and "While You Work" appeared on buses as part of the Shared Spaces / Shared Voices public art project in Indianapolis. "Hunger" appears in the anthology *Irrepressible Appetites* (Rock Press, 2003), edited by Tracey Broussard.